Celebrations Around the World

by Helen Gregory

Consultant:
Adria F. Klein, PhD
California State University, San Bernardino

Wonder Readers are published by Capstone Press,
1710 Roe Crest Drive, North Mankato, Minnesota 56003.
www.capstonepub.com

Library of Congress Cataloging-in-Publication Data
Gregory, Helen.
  Celebrations around the world / Helen Gregory.
    p. cm.—(Wonder readers)
Includes index.
ISBN 978-1-4765-0040-9 (library binding)
ISBN 978-1-4296-7799-8 (paperback)
ISBN 978-1-4765-0853-5 (eBook PDF)
  1. Holidays—Cross-cultural studies—Juvenile literature. 2. Special days—Cross-cultural studies—Juvenile
literature. I. Title.
  GT3933.G75 2013
  394.26—dc23   2011023313

Summary: Describes celebrations and holidays from countries around the world.

Editorial Credits

Maryellen Gregoire, project director; Mary Lindeen, consulting editor; Gene Bentdahl, designer;
Sarah Schuette, editor; Wanda Winch, media researcher; Eric Manske, production specialist

Photo Credits

Capstone Studio: Karon Dubke, 1, 5, 8, 14, 15, 17, 18; Dreamstime: Conny Sjostrom, 12; Shutterstock: Ilya D.
Gridnev, 16, indianstockimages, 6, Noam Armonn, 7, Pavel Losevsky, 4, Roxanne McMillen, 13,
Stanislaw Tokarski, 11, windmoon, cover, 10; Super Stock Inc.: Nordic Photos, 9

Word Count: **245**   Guided Reading Level: **I**   Early Intervention Level: **16**

Printed in China.
092012   006934LEOS13

Table of Contents

Note to Parents and Teachers

The Wonder Readers Next Steps: Social Studies series supports national social studies standards. These titles use text structures that support early readers, specifically with a close photo/text match and glossary. Each book is perfectly leveled to support the reader at the right reading level, and the topics are of high interest. Early readers will gain success when they are presented with a book that is of interest to them and is written at the appropriate level.

Fall Celebrations

In fall, Germans celebrate in October
to honor a king's wedding day.
They listen and dance to polka music.

Americans celebrate Thanksgiving in November. People give thanks by eating a special meal to celebrate the **harvest**.

People celebrate Diwali in India.
Hindu people light small oil lamps
in their homes.

Rosh Hashanah celebrates the Jewish New Year. Jewish families eat apples with honey.

Winter Celebrations

In America, some people celebrate Kwanzaa during the winter. Families learn about African **culture** and values.

On December 13th, Swedish people celebrate a festival of light. Girls dress up as Saint Lucia and carry candles.

Chinese people celebrate the Chinese New Year. The dragon dance brings good luck.

People in Poland and in other countries celebrate Three Kings Day. They dress up as characters from the Christmas story.

Spring Celebrations

Families in Sweden dance around a maypole on May Day. The maypole is decorated with ribbons and flowers to welcome spring.

Cambodians celebrate the New Year in spring. People dance and watch parades with their families and friends.

Mexicans celebrate Cinco de Mayo.
Children hit **piñatas**. Dancers wear
colorful costumes.

Earth Day is celebrated on April 22 around the world. People plant trees and learn to protect our planet.

Summer Celebrations

Tanabata is a Japanese star festival. People write their wishes on strips of paper and hang them on bamboo branches.

On July 4th, Americans celebrate their **independence**. They go camping, have picnics, and watch fireworks.

We all have special days to celebrate.
What's your favorite?

Now Try This!

Think about a special day you celebrate in your home, school, or community. Write a short description of how you celebrate that special day. Draw a picture or cut out photos from magazines that show the clothing, food, or other items you use to mark this holiday. Put the pictures and your description of the holiday in a scrapbook to share with your friends.

Glossary

culture   a people's way of life, ideas, customs, and traditions

harvest   crops that are gathered when they are ripe

independence   freedom from the control of other people or things

piñata   a hollow, decorated container filled with candy or toys; people try to break the piñata with a stick

Internet Sites

FactHound offers a safe, fun way to find Internet sites related to this book. All of the sites on FactHound have been researched by our staff.

Here's all you do:

Visit *www.facthound.com*

Type in this code: 9781476500409

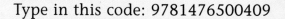

Super-cool stuff! Check out projects, games and lots more at **www.capstonekids.com**

Index